To Lea

 # CELTIC
BLESSINGS
FOR EVERYDAY LIFE

Hope this book
gives you untold
blessings home
Doris

CELTIC BLESSINGS

FOR EVERYDAY LIFE

Prayers for
Every Occasion

Compiled by
RAY SIMPSON

Hodder & Stoughton
LONDON SYDNEY AUCKLAND

British Library Cataloguing in Publication Data.
A record for this book is available from the British Library.

ISBN 0 340 71421 2

Printed and bound in Great Britain by
Mackays of Chatham PLC, Chatham, Kent.

Hodder and Stoughton Ltd
A Division of Hodder Headline PLC
338 Euston Road
London NW1 3BH

....

Other books by Ray Simpson
published by Hodder & Stoughton Ltd:
Exploring Celtic Spirituality: Historic Roots for our Future
Celtic Worship Through the Year
Celtic Daily Light

I dedicate this book
to three people
who have been such blessings to me
that without them
this book could never have been written:
Barbara, Sally and Steven.

They undergird the work of Lindisfarne Mustard Seed Project
(registered charity no. 1054649) which works in association with the
Community of Aidan and Hilda. If you would like to support or use its
ministry, please write to:

Lindisfarne Mustard Seed Project
Community of Aidan and Hilda.
Lindisfarne Retreat
Holy Island
Berwick upon Tweed
TD15 2SD.

CONTENTS

INTRODUCTION

Our society believes in the greatest choice for the greatest number of people. So why should we limit blessings to a few formal occasions in Church? God likes everyone!

It is time to put some meaning back into that time-honoured British phrase 'And every blessed thing'. Why *shouldn't* everything be blessed? Our forbears, the Celts, had blessings for just about everything, from getting dressed to milking the cow. Home life, work life, travel, birth and death and everything in between got blessed.

The Christian Bible scholar Claus Westermann reminds us that God deals with his people in two main ways[i], by delivering them from what is bad and by blessing what is good in their lives: 'So the LORD brought us out of Egypt with a mighty hand and an outstretched arm, . . . He brought us to this place and gave us this land, a land flowing with milk and honey; . . .' (*Deuteronomy 26:8-9, NIV*). In the Old Testament, blessing included both the spiritual and the material aspects of life. Another scholar reminds us that 'Blessing is life, health, and fertility for the people, their cattle, their fields . . . blessing is the basic power of life itself'.[ii] Abraham, whom Christians, Jews and Muslims call their spiritual father, has his entire vocation carved out for him in terms of blessing. We read in the book of Genesis, chapter 12, verses 1 to 4, that he is told by God:

> Go from your country and your kindred and your father's house to the land that I will show you. I will make of you a great nation, and I will bless you, and make your name great, so that you will be a blessing. I will bless those who bless

you, and the one who curses you I will curse;
and in you all the families of the earth shall be
blessed. So Abram went, as the LORD had told
him.

(NRSV adapted)

When Jacob gave his final blessings to the twelve clans that had
begun to grow out of his twelve sons he gave each one a
blessing that was appropriate to his character and
circumstances (*Genesis 49*). Blessings of a whole tribe were
passed on through a father to his sons.

We can learn two important lessons from this. First, blessing is
mediated along the lines of relationship. Once relationships
are severed the blessing is dissipated. To go around blessing
people or objects in a perfunctory way is magic, it is not of God.
Secondly, the work of blessing is most effective when it is
linked with knowledge, wisdom, or the gift of 'seeing' which
Jacob possessed.

Christ demonstrated the dual work of deliverance and blessing,
and he asked his apostles to continue a work of 'binding and
loosing' (i.e. blessing) people (*Matthew 16:19*). Christ's final act
before his ascension was to bless his assembled apostles (*Luke
24:50-51*). This action gave them a visible sign of his earlier
promise: 'I am with you always, to the end of the age.'
(*Matthew 28:20, NRSV*). It served as a model for the blessing
which is bestowed by others in the name of Christ - such as
pastors, parents, friends. Through the hands of the apostles and
their successors the Lord continues to bless his people even
now.

Why, then, have we lost sight of the importance of blessing in
all aspects of life? Since Augustine, the influential 4th. century
church theologian, there has been a tendency in western
Christianity to emphasise the evil in human life from which we
need deliverance, but to fail to emphasise the good in human
life and in creation which we need to bless. This is like looking
at the world through spectacles which have only one lens. If

one only looks at the world to see what is wrong with it, without also looking to see what is right with it, a jaundiced outlook sets in. By using spectacles with the lens of sin but without the lens of goodness, the theology and the practice of blessing has been lost sight of. Yet it is an essential part of our biblical birthright which we need to recover.

Fortunately, the Celtic Church, like the Orthodox Church today, never forgot the value of blessing, and the resurgence of Celtic Christianity helps to restore blessing to us.

The Celtic and the Orthodox Churches never forgot that it is Christ, not his representative, who gives the blessing. To bestow a blessing an Orthodox priest's fingers are arranged to form the letters ICXC, an abbreviation in Greek letters for 'Jesus Christ'. This signifies that the blessing is Christ's, not that of a mere human.

The pre-Christian Celts used to call down blessings from the sun on all sorts of everyday things. As they said a blessing they made a circle with their hands in the direction of the sun as it moved from its rising in the east to its setting in the west. The Christians took this as a good instinct, but gave their blessings in the name of the Triune God, who created the sun. They called the making of a circle the Caim, which they did three times, once each in the name of the Father, the Son and the Spirit, often referred to as The Three. In this way, everything under the sun was blessed, encircled and protected.

Brigid of Ireland was a great blesser, and a potent symbol of blessing. Through her, God mediated compassion, energy, fertility, healing. She often helped her mother, who, though a Christian, was a hard-working slave of a druid priest. A song she sang as she churned the butter begins 'Mary's Son, my friend, come to bless this kitchen. May we have fulness through you.' Through Brigid the Lord multiplied the butter as once he multiplied the loaves and fishes. The following prayer from the *Carmina Gadelica* [iii] always brings to mind Brigid in her kitchen:

You who put beam in moon and sun,
You who put food in ear and herd,
You who put fish in stream and sea,
Send the butter up to me.
Come, you rich lumps, come!
Come, you rich lumps, come!
Come, you rich lumps. masses large,
Come, you rich lumps, come!

At Columba's monastery on Iona every person on the island, and the animals, walked sunwise round the Angels Hill on Michaelmas Day to bring a blessing on the island for the coming year.

Columba blessed all sorts of things with the sign of the cross: the cows' milking pail, the work tools, the pen that the writing might be to the glory of God, the seed that the crops might be saved from harm.

The blessing and prayers of the western highlanders of Scotland collected in the 19th century by Alexander Carmichael (the *Carmina Gadelica*), carry on this tradition. Nothing is too earthy or too small to be included in a blessing. Not only is each cow included but each teat as well!

The *Carmina Gadelica* recounts the story of a poor little old woman whose husband had died and whose son had drowned. She was left with three orphans to care for but her heifer would neither produce milk nor calf. She sought Columba's help. Columba made up a song of blessing which he sang to her heifer with tears streaming down his cheeks, and then he taught her to sing it too:

My heifer, beloved, be not alone
Let your little calf be before you.

Coax your pretty one to yourself
Till you send to the fold a herd.

Certain is the gentle proverb
The cow of blessings is the cow of calves.

The black heifer is reconciled
You will be lowing to your pretty one.

You will come home with droves
You will quench the thirst of hundreds.

The poor woman crooned this blessing to her heifer and the cow took to her calf. This is an example of a prophetic blessing, like the blessings of Jacob in the Bible. The prayer of faith calls forth what is being blessed in words so that it becomes a reality.

Catherine Maclennon, one of the highlanders who passed on to Alexander Carmichael the words of blessings which had become part of the fabric of their lives once told him:

> My mother would be asking us to sing our morning song to God down in the back-house, as Mary's lark was singing it up in the clouds and as Christ's mavis was singing it yonder in the tree, giving glory to the God of the creatures for the repose of the night, for the light of the day, and for the joy of life. She would tell us that every creature on the earth here below and in the ocean beneath and in the air above was giving glory to the great God of the creatures and the worlds, of the virtues and the blessings, and would *we* be dumb!

HOW TO USE THIS BOOK

There are blessings in this book for every aspect of our lives today. The first section contains specific blessings for everyday events. See the contents list to find one that is appropriate as you need it.

The second section responds to requests for Celtic touches to formal occasions such as infant blessings, baptisms, house blessings, weddings. Some of these are in the form of services, others are to complement the normal services. It is best to read the services through first, and choose the sections that you wish to use before you make the arrangements with family, friends, and any clergy. You will need to decide beforehand whether to invite a minister or a soul friend (i.e. a friend who has a spiritual rapport with what you will pledge in the service) to help lead the service. Where a space is left blank, then the name of the person for whom blessing is sought (or the parent/sibling etc.) should be inserted.

The third section is for routine use and contains blessings for different times of each day and for different seasons of each year.

The final section has blessings for personal use at significant stages in one's journey through life.

Throughout the book, you can apply a blessing to yourself rather than to others by interchanging 'you' for 'me' etc.

Ray Simpson
Lindisfarne Retreat
Holy Island TD15 2SD

NOTES

[i] Westermann, Claus, *Blessing in the Bible and the Life of the Church*, Philadelphia, 1978, pp. 1-15, quoted in Fox, Matthew, *Original Blessing*, Bear & Co., 1983

[ii] Mowinckel, Sigmund, *The Psalms in Israel's Worship*, Blackwell, 1967, vol. 2, p. 44, trans. D.R. Ap-Thomas

[iii] Carmichael, Alexander (Ed.), *Carmina Gadelica*, Floris Books, Edinburgh, 1992, p. 341

1

EVERYDAY BLESSINGS

A LONELY SOUL

In the stillness

See the wonder of God's art

In the silence

Feel Christ's presence

In the sunlight

Watch the Holy Spirit dance

In the darkness

Find faith's essence.

Jane M. Machickan

COMPUTERS

I programme my computer

with the love of God.

God be with me now

as I call words into being.

May they make real my work of love.

May they join the work of creation.

Called from nothing, uttered over chaos

bringing order.

Esther de Waal

THE CREATION

Also to be prayed when astronauts visit other planets.

Dear planet
The Light of all light shine on you
The Power of all power energise you
The Love of all love win you.

May you become aware
that the Eternal Three
caress without ceasing
all forms, all realities
with graces, energies
and creative manifestations.

May you be unhindered by human egotism.

May consciousness of the One in Three dawn upon you.
May co-operation with the Three develop upon you.
May you move forward into your divine destiny.

EXAMS

Every exam subject, whether it be art or language, domestic science or computer technology, reflects something of the nature of God. As we name and bless a forthcoming exam, we relax and this helps to bring out the best in us.

I bless this exam

in the name of the Designer of truth

I bless this exam

in the name of the Protector from ill

I bless this exam

in the name of the Spirit who guides.

Open my eyes to see how this subject

reflects something of you.

Aid me to understand this subject

with my heart as well as with my head.

Give me

Wisdom to know the nub of things

Strength to recall what is useful

Peace to leave the result to you.

FAMILY

FATHERS

God help you to
listen to your loved ones
play with your loved ones
laugh with your loved ones
weep with your loved ones
forgive your loved ones
take responsibility for your loved ones
be faithful to your loved ones
for ever.

Bless you fathers,
May you be priests
to your wives and children.

MOTHER

Mother, dear,
pearl of great price,
too often have we taken you for granted.

May the Holy Trinity protect you
May the Three of limitless love renew you

so that

An island shall you be in our seas
A light shall you be in our nights
A well shall you be in our deserts
until Heaven's arms enfold you, too.

GRANDPARENT

May this little one bring
Love and affection to you
And good to the earth.

May this be a day of grace for you.

May you be a guarding one to this gift of heaven
Along with the saints and the angels
and the Three of limitless love.

MISCARRIAGE

Bible readings

Some people brought little children to Jesus for
him to place his hands on them, but the disciples
scolded the people. When Jesus noticed this he was
angry and said to the disciples: 'Let the little ones
come to me, and do not stop them, because the
kingdom of God belongs to such as these.'

Mark 10:13, 14

Jesus said: 'See that you don't despise any of these
little ones. Their angels in heaven, I tell you, are
always in the presence of my good Father in
heaven.' *Matthew 18:10*

A Parent's Prayer

Dear Lord Jesus, kind and loving Friend, you were always glad
to be in the company of children; you taught us that we must
be like them in the kingdom of heaven. I now realise that I
have more children than at first it seemed.

The child who was lost through miscarriage is mine and yours.

I give this child the name *N*...............................
I pray that you will heal the scars of *N*... *[name of the child]*
May *N*... *[name of the child]* be enfolded in your love.

May *s/he* find healing.

Set *N*... *free* from all shock or hurt that hinders their journey
into wholeness in your kingdom, so that *N*... may live with you
in light and joy for ever. I look forward to that day when,
through faith in Jesus Christ, we may be reunited in paradise.

A minister or friend's prayer for the deceased child[ren]

We release *N*... into your hands. May your blessing and your
peace be upon *N*... Bring *him/her* to wholeness in your eternal
kingdom.

BATTERED PEOPLE

Gentle Father
Bless these battered children.
Take the hurt out of their lives.
May your gentle spirit flow
through all those who care for them.

Tender Saviour
Bless these battered wives
Take the fear out of their lives.
May your tender spirit flow
through all those who care for them.

Caressing Spirit
Bless these elderly who feel battered
by their children's rejection.
Take resentment out of their lives.
May your caressing spirit flow
through all those who care for them.

STEPCHILDREN

The family of God to draw round you
The family of God to welcome you
The family of God to listen to you
The family of God to cherish you
The family of God to heal you
Mary the mother of our Lord
Joseph at his work
All the saints of heaven
Your guardian angels
And we your new loved ones.

May heaven's gates of welcome open wide
May our heart of welcome open wide
May your heart of welcome open wide
This day and always.

TODDLER

To be said when washing the toddler

The three palmfuls of the Sacred Three
To preserve you from every envy or evil eye:
The palmful of the Father of life;
The palmful of the Christ of love;
The palmful of the Spirit of peace,
The God of threefold love.

FRIENDS

Beauty of friendship grow between us
Friendship
without guile
without malice
without striving.

Goodness of friendship grow between us
Friendship
with light
with wings
with soul sharing.

Be in the eye of each friend
of my journey
to bless and to teach each one.

The eye of the Father be upon us
The eye of the Son be upon us
The eye of the Spirit be upon us
The eye of the Friendly Three
be upon us for ever.

GARDENS

*It is good to bless a new garden, a re-landscaped
garden, or even a new season for a garden.*

There is no plant in the ground
That does not tell of your beauty, Lord.
May this garden speak to us of the fragrance of your love.
May the fruits of the earth speak to us of your mercy.

Bless the moon that is above us;
The earth that is beneath us;
The hard work to be done here;
The seedlings that shall grow here;
The neighbours we shall greet here;
And all who overlook here.

HOLIDAYS

Blessing of sun be yours
Blessing of earth be yours
Blessing of rock be yours
Blessing of sky be yours
Blessing of wind be yours
Blessing of water be yours
Blessing of fun be yours
Blessing of stillness be yours
Blessing of discovery be yours
Blessing of rest be yours
Blessing of meeting be yours
Blessing of thought be yours
Blessing of change be yours
Blessing of homecoming be yours.

home

WHEN AWAY FROM HOME

*Don't take worries about those left behind, release them. These prayers
can help in doing this.*

We release into your hands, O Lord, our homes
Those whom we love and care for
Any who are dependent on us who may feel vulnerable
without us.
Lord, you love those whom we love.

We release into your hands, O Lord,
Those for whom we have responsibilities
Those who are in need at this time
Those we have supported.
Lord, you care for all those for whom we care.

We release into your hands, O Lord, our work
The pressures that weary us
The problems that would pursue us
The things we have forgotten
The tasks left unfinished.
Lord, you rule over all things.

ARRIVING IN A NEW PLACE

Lord, we offer you our conflicting feelings
Our apprehensions and our aspirations,
The strange bed, the changed roles, the fear of the
unknown.

Risen Christ, we acknowledge that you are in our midst,
Circle this place and make it your own
Keep peace within, keep evil out.
May all memories, influences or powers that are not of
you flee from this place
May the angels guard and welcome us.

We turn our eyes upon you,
Calm us and settle us
Help us to feel at home with you and with one another
So there is no need to pretend.
Help us to be ourselves
And to see these news faces as our family.

ON RETURNING HOME

God of the fray, God of the bumps
Cool me down, because I am frayed.
Lift me up, because I have come down with a bump.
Help me to accept the duties that confront me.
Help me to assimilate the experiences that have enriched me
And to become aware of your presence
Now in the present moment.

INFERTILITY

Call forth life within us.

Father of life
Bless the swarming sperm
that teems with life so manifold.
Spirit of life
Bless the welcoming egg
that patiently waits to conceive.
Saviour of Life
Change the barren water of this womb
into a wine-like ferment of life.

Call forth life within us.

Bless to us, O God, the anguish that is ours.
Change the stagnant void in our hearts
into a life-giving stream
That we may become pregnant with fresh creativity
Love pouring forth abundantly from us
Mothering and fathering an orphaned world
Bringing to flower the seeds you have planted in us
Faith and joy outpouring.

ILLNESS AND INJURY

TALKING TO THE DISEASED ORGAN

Jesus sometimes spoke in a direct, pithy way to a disease. 'Be clean' (of leprosy) Matthew 8:8; 'come out' (of a demon) Luke 4:35; 'wash'; (to cure blindness) John 9:7. These prayers, mostly from the Carmina Gadelica, *direct God's power to a particular part of the anatomy.*

To N... *[name the affected organ]:*
The God of gods
The Healer of healers,
The Spirit of eternity,
The perfect Three of power
Restore you.

To a stye:
Go back! go back! go back!
You thievish rascal of the stye!

For the removal of a microbe in the body:
May God search for them, may God remove them
From your blood, from your flesh, from your urine,
From your smooth fragrant bones;
From your close veins, from your hard kidney,
From your pith, from your marrow, dear one,
From this day and every day
Till the day you shall end your life.

To a blind or affected eye while bathing or touching it:

Pour, King of life,

Pour, Christ of peace,

Pour Spirit of cleansing.

You who created the orb

And placed the pupil in the eye,

Search the mystery within the lid,

Befriend its sight, O God.

Make whole this day the eye;

Restore this day the sight.

When laying hands on a painful part of the body:

Power of heaven have I over you;

Power of universe have I over you;

Power of sun have I over you;

Power of earth have I over you;

Power of God have I over you.

Powers of God, work God's will in you.

For any disease of the body:

May the strong Lord of life
Destroy your disease of body
From the crown of your head
To the base of your heel.
With the power of the Christ of love
And the Creator of the seasons,
With the aid of the Holy Spirit,
And the powers of wholeness together.

For a swelling:

Peace come into this swelling,
The peace of the King of power.
Subsiding come to your swelling.

Look, O Christ, on this swelling,
Since you are the King of power
Give rest to this person.
Bring the microbe out of this tumour.
Be whole. Let your swelling now shrink.
In the holy presence of the Father,
In the holy presence of the Son,
In the holy presence of the Spirit,
The holy presence of compassion.

For any skin or blood disease:

May God heal you, my dear one.
I am now placing my hand on you
In the name of Father, Son, and Spirit of virtue,
Three Persons who encompass you for ever.
Full healing come to your blood,
Perfect healing to your soft flesh,
Another healing to your smooth skin,
In the name of the powers of the Holy Three.

For a removal of a disease of the spirit:

As Christ removed the sleep from the little child of the grave,
May he remove from you, dear one,
Each frown, each envy, each malice.

When a person suffers from insecurity or a lack of identity:

An eye was seeing you,
A mouth has named you,
A heart has thought of you,
A mind has desired you:

ILLNESS AND INJURY (CONTD)

THE HEALING RHYTHM OF THE TRINITY

*A common Celtic practice is to perform a healing action three times,
which reflects the healing rhythm of the Trinity:*

I commend you, N... *[name the sick person]*
In the eye of God,
In the love of Jesus,
In the name of Spirit,
In Trinity of power.

May Three Persons sanctify you,
May Three Persons help you,
The Father and the Son
And the perfect Spirit.

HEALING WITH WATER

*Water is placed in a bowl; a leaf or sponge is dipped in it and placed on
the affected part with words such as these:*

May this water be for your healing
In the holy name of the Father,
In the holy name of the Son,
In the holy name of the Spirit,
In the holy name of the Three,
Everlasting, kindly, wise.

INJURY

I am appealing to you, since you are the King of heaven
I am praying to you, since you are the King of good
Lift each wasting, each weariness and sickness.

Lift each soreness and discomfort
I am keenly praying to you
Lift each stiffness
As you separate earth from ocean.

LOSS

All of us experience loss in one way or another, for it can come in many forms. We may suffer, for example, loss of children, health, home, job, limb, or spouse.

Bruised?
The blessing of acceptance be yours.

Bitter?
The blessing of forgiveness be yours.

Angry?
The blessing of gentleness be yours.

Suicidal?
The blessing of trust be yours.

Broken?
The blessing of immortality be yours.

MONEY

Many of us receive money weekly or monthly, either directly or paid into an account. Sometimes we receive an extra or unexpected sum of money. We call such money a 'windfall'. This windfall can be either a blessing or a curse, so it is important to bring it to God from the first.

Good be on you, gift from heaven
Wisdom be on you, gift from heaven
Restraint be on you, gift from heaven
Thought be on you, gift from heaven
The Giver be on you, gift from heaven
Jesus be on you, gift from heaven
The Spirit be on you, gift from heaven

Now you have begun the practice of blessing special amounts of money, why not practice this blessing of money whenever you receive your regular income?

PARTIES AND NIGHTS OUT

Circle us, Lord
Keep these graces within:
The grace of form
The grace of beauty
The grace of movement
The grace of eating
The grace of conversation
The grace of laughter
The grace of listening
The grace of restraint
The grace of self-forgetfulness.

Circle us, Lord
Keep these evils without:
The evil of fear
The evil of boasting
The evil of pretence
The evil of excess
The evil of abuse
The evil of addiction.

PETS

Many people have repeated the blessing St. Brigid of Ireland used to place upon her calves, goats, horses and lambs. The following blessings for pets reflect this:

Each day and each night
In cold and heat
In light and dark
Keep them from falling
Keep them from road accidents
Keep them from thieves
Keep them from poisons
Keep them content
O sweet Maker of all.

N... *[name of pet]*,
the eye of God be on you
to bless you
to look after you
to give you pleasure
and to make you a pleasure.

PLANTS

There is no plant in the ground
But is full of your virtue
O King of the virtues.
May these plants bring your blessing to us.

There is no life in the earth
But proclaims your goodness.
O King of goodness
May these plants bring your goodness to us.

As I look at their leaves turned face to the sun
May I look towards you until this day is done.
As I admire the bright flowers
Giving glory to you
May I bring you pleasure in the things that I do
As I look at the fruit tasty and sweet
May I taste of you to the people I meet.
Craig Roberts

SPORTING ACHIEVEMENT

*This is a suitable prayer to present on a card or to say on return home
after someone has completed a marathon, won a medal, or been part of
a team which has competed in a competition.*

We bless you, God, for the goodness of this achievement.

The strength of the ox be yours
The speed of a gazelle be yours
The suppleness of fish be yours
The flight of a bird be yours
The joy of the earth be yours
The warmth of the sun be yours.

The wreath of God around your neck
The wreath of God around your chest
The wreath of God around your thighs
The wreath of God around your feet

And the gold everlasting.

TRANSPORT

CAR

Bless this car to me O Lord
Bless me to my car.
Be in my driving
Be in my concentration
Be in my decisions.

Bless this journey to me, O Lord.
It is a small reflection of my journey through life,
My way chosen by you.
A journey with you
A journey to you.
A journey to knowing myself
A journey to knowing you
A journey of being saved and healed.

Bless the people I drive by, O Lord.
May they be aware of you in this place.
Bless the owners of the businesses,
May they deal justly and honestly.
Bless the schools, polytechnics and universities.
Give a teachable spirit to both pupil and teacher.

Carole Parker

NEW BICYCLE

Good speed to you
Good balance to you
Good movement to you.

Power of air to you
Power of wheel to you
Power of frame to you.

Grace of a grateful heart to you
In the name of God
of the starting out
and of the good returning.

NEW CAR

May it bless the earth it will travel on
May it bless the earth that fuels it
May it bless each one who enters it
May it bless each one it passes.

May it be used wisely
May it rest until it is needed
May it be a humble gift to the world
May it be a sign of our good God.
May it go well and be well
Each day and each night of its time.

NEWCAR(contd)

To the owner or user:

May this be a gift of space to you
May this be a gift of movement to you
May this be a gift of sight to you
May this be a gift of meeting to you
In the name of the God
who makes and moves all things.

NEW MOTORCYCLE

God bless your steed
God bless your speed
Christ meet your need.

By the Spirit be led
And angels overhead
Until you reach your bed.

TRAVEL

God bless the path on which you go
God bless the earth beneath your feet
God bless your destination.

God be a smooth way before you
A guiding star above you
A keen eye behind you
This day, this night, and for ever.

God be with you whatever you pass
Jesus be with you whatever you climb
Spirit be with you wherever you stay.

God be with you at each stop and each sea
At each lying down and each rising up
In the trough of the waves, on the crest of the billows
Each step of the journey you take.

WORK AND CAREER

May my work be faithful
May my work be honest
May my work be blessed
May my work bless others
May my work bless you.

May the wealth and work of the world
be available to all
and for the exploitation of none.

May managers, employees and shareholders work
together like fingers on a hand.

JOINING UP

It is a mistake to reserve prayers only for the 'nice' aspects of life. Some people are called to serve in the Armed Services, in Emergency Services, or in a political or campaigning movement that is far from cosy.

The first three requests in the following blessing come from the motto of Ireland's
'Fianna'.

May you have
truth in your hearts
strength in your hands
consistency in your tongues
and love in your being.

NEW JOB

Bless to me, O God, everything my eye shall see
Bless to me, O God, everything my hand shall do
Bless to me, O God, everything my brain shall think
Bless to me, O God, the place and the equipment.
Bless to me, O God, the people we shall serve through
our work

Be in the interruptions and the setbacks
Be in the eye of the person who is difficult
Be in the eye of the person who is a delight.

NEW TASK

*When we begin some new task, whether it is voluntary or paid, it is
good to make a re-dedication of ourselves to God, with others.*

Speaker   In blessing our foreheads
All   **we reclaim the powers of reason**

Speaker   In blessing our eyes
All   **we reclaim the power of vision**

Speaker   In blessing our lips
All   **we reclaim the power to speak**

Speaker   In blessing our hands
All   **we reclaim the power of creativity**

Speaker   In blessing our feet
All   **we reclaim the power of movement**

PROMOTION

A proportion of us are promoted or invited to accept some office of greater responsibility at one time or another. This may be in national or local government, in education, business, media, church or elsewhere. This, too, should be marked before God and before one's family.

This blessing reflects advice from Cormac, who was known as the Irish Solomon, to those who were to become kings or warriors. Cormac observed that it was through these habits that the young could become kingly.

God's blessing be upon you for this new office.
May you be
Not too conceited or you will lose the bonds of trust
Not too naive or you will be deceived
Not too diffident or you will fail to convince
Not too talkative or you will not be heard
Not too silent or you will not be heeded
Not too hard or you will be broken
Not too feeble or you will be disregarded.

REDUNDANCY

Bless to me, O God,
this loss, that I may grow through grieving
this worry, that I may learn through trusting
this space, that I may develop through creating
this grim bureaucrat, that I may become gracious through bearing.

God bless to you this loss
that you may know the eternal boss.
God bless you in being poor
that Providence will open its door.
God bless to you this 'grave'
that you may know that Christ can save.

11
FORMAL
OCCASIONS

NOTES

In this section some preparation is needed: the appropriate sections of services need to be chosen; responses need to be ticked or made a note of (in the Service of Infant Blessing for example); blanks need to be filled in; choices made between *her/him* and *her/his* etc.

Where it is suggested that everyone present speaks certain words, these are printed in bold with 'All' before them.

BAPTISM

FOR A SERVICE OF INFANT BAPTISM
IN A CHURCH

When family and friends have gathered someone may sing a song, and a minister or someone similar explains the meaning of baptism. The church's large Easter candle is lit for use in the service.

THE SIGNING OF THE FOREHEAD WITH THE
SIGN OF THE CROSS

The minister or the person baptising says:

I mark you with the sign of the cross

The sign of the cross is made on the baby's forehead

In Brittany, at the Cathedral of the Celtic St. Samson of Dol, I saw each member of the baby's family and its godparents in turn make the sign of the cross on the baby's forehead. Everyone says words such as the following:

All   **May the cross of Christ always be between you and the evil powers;**

       May the cross of Christ always be between you and all ill-will and mishap;

       May the cross of Christ always be between you and everything dark or shameful;

       May the cross of Christ always be between you and all that hurts or harms your soul.

GOD'S WORDS

As at St. Samson's Cathedral, it is good if the family can take an active part. So an older brother, sister or relative now reads from the Bible . . .

GOD'S CALLING TO PARENTS

Parents may offer encouragement by way of stories or testimonies about how they make the baptism vows real for their children. One mother may tell of how she prays with her infant, a father may say how he prays with and listens to his child.

BLESSING THE BABY'S FUTURE

A person may give a flower, plant or anything beautiful and natural and say to the parents:

Today we ask that you will try to make your home beautiful, so that your child may grow up to appreciate God's beauty.

And to the child:

So today we give you N... *[name of child]* this beautiful flower and pray that the personality God has given you will flower into its full beauty.

A person may give a crafted object and say to the parents:

Today we ask that you will try to make your home reflect something of the Creator, by expressing the creativity God has given you and others.

And to the child:

So today we give you N... *[name of child]* this crafted present, and pray that the creativity God has given you may be fully used.

A person may give to the parents a Bible or book of prayers and say:

Today we ask that you will try in your home to learn about Jesus and to listen to God's voice in the Bible and in your hearts

And to the child:

So we give you N... *[name of child]* this Bible (or book) and pray that you will find and follow your calling.

The minister or another person may give to a parent, on behalf of the baby, a candle which they first light from the church's large Easter candle which should have been lit and placed nearby before the service, saying

Today we ask that you will make your home a place of faith which radiates the light of Christ.

And to the child:

So we give you N... *[name of child]* this candle and pray that you may shine as a light in the world.

All say this prayer:

> **Christ as a light illumine and guide you**
>
> **Christ as a shield overshadow you**
>
> **Christ under you**
>
> **Christ over you**
>
> **Christ beside you on your left and your right**
>
> **This day be within and without you**
>
> **Lonely and meek yet all powerful**
>
> **Be in the mouth of each to whom you shall speak**
>
> **In the mouth of each who shall speak to you**
>
> **Christ as a light illumine and guide you.**

St. Patrick's Breastplate, adapted

As the water is poured three times over the baby, the prayer for birth 'A little drop of your Creator' on page 97 may be used.

BAPTISM OF BELIEVERS

This prayer may be said immediately before the person goes into the water, or immediately after the baptism while they are still in the water.

Into the life of the Father I immerse you

That he may protect you from harm

Bring you peace and calm

Into the boundless life of your Maker I immerse you.

Into the life of the Son I immerse you

That he may save you from hell

Keep you washed and well.

Into the sinless life of your Saviour I immerse you.

Into the life of the Spirit I immerse you

That the Spirit may light up your night

And give you power to do right

Into the endless life of your Soul Friend I immerse you.

Into the life of the Three I immerse you

That they may fill you with love

Lift you to heaven above.

Into the selfless love of the Trinity I immerse you.

FUNERAL

A Dead Citizen's Charter recently called for people to take funerals back into their own hands. Why should they be packaged, impersonal rites from which all poetry, feeling and 'flow' has fled?

BEFORE THE FUNERAL

The Irish Wake, at which friends and family gather together around the coffin for food, music and recounting of memories, retains the Celtic idea of celebrating a life.

It can be a healing experience to keep the dead person's body in a place where friends and family can see it, sit by it, and put flowers or mementos on it. Some people will wish to be silent, others may wish to say a blessing such as this:

Go to your eternal home of welcome my loved companion.

Go into the sleep of Jesus

The restoring sleep of Jesus

The young sleep of Jesus.

Go into the kiss and the peace and the glory of Jesus

Into the arms of the Jesus of blessings

Into the generous Christ with his hands around you.

Drawing near to the Trinity

Freed from your pains

Pardoned from your sins

Christ beside you bringing peace to your mind.

FUNERAL (CONTD)

AT THE FUNERAL

If the deceased person had been baptised, you may ask for water to be sprinkled over the coffin before the cremation or burial; and you may ask for words such as these to be spoken:

May you who were baptised N... *[state the deceased person's baptismal names]*

now be immersed into the life of God:

Into the presence of the Creator I immerse you

Into the presence of the Saviour I immerse you

Into the presence of the Spirit I immerse you.

At the funeral service, prayers such as these may be included:

May kindly Michael, chief of the holy angels,
Take charge of your beloved soul
And tenderly bring it home
To the Three of limitless love:
Creator, Saviour, Eternal life-giver.

FUNERAL (CONTD)

Father, I place N... into your hands;
Acknowledge a sheep of your own fold,
A lamb of your own flock,
A sinner of your own redeeming.
Enfold N... in the arms of your mercy,
In the blessed rest of everlasting peace,
And in the glorious company of the saints in light.

Traditional

Go forth upon your journey from this world,
In the Name of God the Father who created you;
In the Name of Jesus Christ who died for you;
In the Name of the Holy Spirit who shines through you;
In friendship with God's saints;
Aided by the holy angels.
May you rest this day in
the peace and love of your eternal home.

Traditional, adapted

May you be as free as the wind
As soft as sheep's wool
As straight as an arrow
That you may journey into the heart of God

FUNERAL (CONTD)
AFTER THE FUNERAL

*Grieving, like life itself, is a process. At the funeral we say 'good-bye',
but afterwards, we often get more fully in touch with feelings, regrets,
longings, memories.*

*The following prayer can be used at an official memorial service, or we
can make our own less formal memorial services at any time, by
finding a quiet space, lighting a candle, looking at a photograph and
slowly, with long pauses, repeating the following prayer.*

Holy God, holy and mighty
You alone are Creator
You alone are Saviour
You alone are immortal.

We are mortal
formed from the earth
returning to the earth
for you ordained
that we should come from dust and go to dust.
Yet through Christ you ordained also
that with our tears at the dark night of parting
should be mingled the Alleluias
of the glory that pierces the gloom from beyond.
So as we remember the shadows
and as we linger with our precious memories:
May we feel your presence
May we be touched by your hope
May we be changed by your glory.

HOLY COMMUNION

For a complete Celtic Holy Communion which can be integrated with the prescribed Order for Holy Communion in the Church of England, please see pp.75-81 of Celtic Worship Through the Year *also by Ray Simpson.*

The blessings here can be incorporated into a standard service. When you receive the bread which represents the body of Christ, or the chalice with the wine in it that represents his blood, remember that these channel the life of Christ to you. This is the blessing of all blessings.

Blessed are you
King of all creation
for this bread
which earth has given and human hands have made.
It will become for me the Bread of Life.

Blessed are you
King of all creation
for this wine
fruit of the vine
work of human hands.
It will become my spiritual drink.

Lamb of God
Defenceless Victor
Take from us our sin
Give to us the food of eternal life.

HOLY COMMUNION (CONTD)

This precious nectar is my delight.
From this cup flows warmth for my darkest night.
From you I drink in poise and power
Though I am broken, in a needy hour.
And cup-sharing with me, are rich and poor,
Folk of all kinds, all thirsty for more.

As I eat and drink, help me
to touch your utter, self-giving love.

HOUSE BLESSINGS

At the entrance

May this house be built upon the Rock of rocks, the rock of Christ; so that no onslaught can undermine it, and no ill-wind can unsettle it. May the guardian angel welcome all who enter this place, and repel all that would harm it.

Blessed water may be sprinkled on the door and used to make the sign of the cross upon it with the finger. (This may be repeated in each room.) Inside the sign of the cross is made or a cross is hung in the hall with the following words:

We invite you, O Christ, to be the master of this household and of everything in it.

May the cross of Christ be between you and all that has happened here in the past.

In the kitchen

We consecrate this kitchen to you. May the deep peace of the Son of Mary possess all who work amidst the clatter of this place; may all be done in a spirit of humble service, may all be done as for you. Bless the washing, bring forth fulness in the cooking, put your glory in the working.

In the eating room

Bless this room. May the eating be a celebration of God's goodness. May the feasting be a fellowship with God's friends. As you drink the sweet fruits of creation, may you drink the sweetness of God's life, and be preserved from the poisons of envy.

HOUSE BLESSINGS (CONTD)

A prayer sometimes attributed to St. Brigid, which may be read by a new resident:

I would prepare a feast and be host to the great High King, with all the company of heaven.

The sustenance of pure love be in my house, the roots of repentance in my house. Baskets of love be mine to give, with cups of mercy for all the company. Sweet Jesus, be there with us, with all the company of heaven. May cheerfulness abound in the feast, the feast of the great High King, my host for all eternity.

In a child's room

May the loving Father God always be here with you and make you feel safe. May friendly Jesus always be here with you and make you feel happy. May the kindly Spirit always be here with you to listen to you. May you enjoy their company as you play. May angels look after you when you sleep, and when you dream, and may they help you to wake with a smile on your face.

In each bedroom

In the name of the eternal Father, in the name of the loving Son, in the name of the gentle Spirit, the friendly Three-in-One: bless and make holy this room, and may angels guard all who sleep here. That part of you that did not grow at morning, may it grow at night. That part that did not grow at night, may it grow in the morning.

In a couple's bedroom

In addition to the above:

God give you delight and tenderness in your lying together. God give you peace and forgiveness in your sleeping together.

God give you solitude and freedom to be yourselves for each other.

In a guest room

In addition to the words for each bedroom:

Fill this room with a spirit of hospitality. May each person who sleeps here be enfolded in the loving arms of the Saviour.

In a work or play room

Bless the work, the play or the study done here. Make fruitful the reading, the writing, the planning. May all that is done reflect the peace and order of creation.

Bathroom and toilets

Either of the following:

May all who bathe their bodies here bathe them in the mild rays of the Sun of suns, as Mary bathed Christ in the rich milk of Egypt. The sweetness of Christ be in your mouth as you clean your teeth; the beauty of Christ be upon your face as you comb your hair; the love of Christ flow over you as you wash your frame.

As you look in the mirror may you see
The hands of Mary washing you,
The hands of angels cleansing you,
The hands of the saints straightening you,
The hands of Jesus restoring you.

In the living room

We place into your hands all those who will live together here. May they know that everything here is yours, and that they belong here. May they sense your love here. May the presence of the Three Kindly Persons free each to accept their pain, to grow through each stage of their development, to give space to each other, to express their feelings, to forgive from their hearts, to flower as persons.

HOUSE BLESSINGS (CONTD)

Discerning of spirits

In homes where this is requested. After a silent waiting on God, any spirit or influence is named that is felt to be present and not of God, e.g. a clinical, a restless, an angry, a fearful, an unclean or an evil spirit. Water may be sprinkled, or a short house Communion performed, showing forth the dying, rising and victory of Christ over all powers, past and present, seen and unseen. Words from the Bible, e.g. Philippians 2:1-11, may be read, together with the following:

Almighty Father, victorious Saviour, Holy Spirit, you are stronger than the elements, stronger than the shadows, stronger than the fears, stronger than human wills, stronger than the spirits; we enthrone you in this place and lift you up with our praise.

There may be singing, e.g. 'Jesus we enthrone you'

In the name of the crucified and risen Christ, we set this place free from the power of the past. In the name of Christ we say to all powers that do not reverence him as Lord: be gone from this place. Be gone.

For pets and other creatures near the home

Dear Lord, may all that is here reflect the harmony and wholeness that you want for all creation.

May the cat(s) purr with the pleasure of friendship;

May the dog(s) wag tail(s) with the delight of meetings;

May N... *[name the pet]* be happy and healthy;

May the wild creatures find nature here is friendly;

May the birds find food here and chirp with gladness.

HOUSE BLESSINGS (CONTD)

In (or looking towards) garden or outhouse:

See the blessing of a garden on page 12.

If there is a party, barbecue or social gathering, this Caim prayer is said by all, if appropriate, after walking in a circle round the property:

All **Circle this place by day and by night;**

Circle it in winter, circle it in summer.

Look down upon it with your smile;

Lift it up with your strength.

Keep far from it all that harms;

Keep all that's good within Christ's arms.

May this place be fragrant with the presence of the Lord;

May this place overflow with the gratitude of his people;

May this place echo with the sounds of joy;

May clouds of God's peace envelop it;

God's peace be always here and in those who dwell here.

Let us enjoy his presence now.

All **Amen**

A SERVICE OF INFANT BLESSING

Children need families; they need their mother and, if possible, their father, to make a commitment to them from the beginning. Most parents want their baby to be blessed, but many do not want this to include church involvement, nor do they want to make vows at a baptism which they cannot keep.

This service is for all parents, of any church or none, who wish to give their child their loving commitment and God's blessing. It may also be used by Christian parents who believe their children should not be baptised until they become believers. It may take place in a church, home or in any building. Parents may ask a church minister, or a respected friend (a soul friend or 'anamchara') to lead the service, and to adapt it so that it fits their needs. They may invite friends to be sponsors, or Godparents, if they wish, though this is not essential.

WELCOME

A minister or soul friend says:

We welcome N... and N... *[names of mother and father]*

and join them in giving thanks for the gift of N...

to be their *daughter/son*, and to be a new *brother/sister* for N... *[name(s) of any siblings or step brothers and sisters of the baby].*

We meet on this special day to celebrate the birth and naming of this child, to witness solemn undertakings on *her/his* behalf by *her/his* parents, the support of Godparents, and to ask God's blessing on this precious life.

THANKS

The parents and/or the minister or soul friend may say:

God our Creator, in giving us this child you have shown us your love. We thank you from our hearts for the joy of this child, for the wonder of this life, for a safe delivery, and for the privilege of being parents.

INFANT BLESSING (CONTD)

NAMING

The minister or soul friend asks the parents:

You have brought your child to be welcomed into your circle of family and friends.

What names have you chosen?

The parent(s) state the name(s) N...

The minister, soul friend, or a parent may explain the meaning of the names if this is desired.

COMMITMENTS

I   The minister or soul friend asks the parent(s):

a) Will you care for this child, feed and befriend *her/him*, listen to and play with *her/him*, keep *her/him* safe, and daily share your heart with *her/him*?

Parent(s): I will.

b) Will you help your child, by your example and your teaching, to be honest, to be responsible, and to help others?

Parent(s): I will.

c) Will you respect, encourage, and guide *her/him*, and will you put *her/his* true needs before your pleasure? Will you try to order your lives so that your child will be surrounded by love and goodness?

Parent(s): I will.

d) For the sake of your child, will you remain together and work at being good friends, even in conflict? Will you say sorry when you are wrong and forgive when you are wronged?

Parent(s): I will.

e) Do you dedicate your child to God?

Parent(s): I do.

f) Do you dedicate yourselves to God, and do you promise, by God's help, to provide a Christian home for this child, to pray with your child, to teach your child about Christ, and to encourage your child to know and serve Christ?

Parent(s): I do.

II   **The minister or soul friend asks the Godparent(s):**

a) Will you be a continuing friend to this child, and be ready to help in times of special need?

Godparents: I will.

b) Will you pray for this child, and give *her/him* opportunities to ask questions about your own journey through life?

Godparents: I will.

INFANT BLESSING (CONTD)

III   **The minister or soul friend asks any sisters, brothers or stepsisters and brothers:**

a)   Will you try and be kind and to share things with *her/him* and will you treat *her/his* parents and your parents with respect?

Siblings: I will

IV   **The minister or soul friend asks the grandparent(s):**

a) Will you do your best to give thoughtful support and encouragement as long as you live?

Grandparent(s): I will.

The minister or soul friend says:

God bless you and help you to carry out these promises.

WORDS TO REMEMBER

The minister or soul friend says:

When the people of Israel were first given guidance as to how to bring up their families, they were told:

> Israel remember this! The LORD – and the LORD alone – is your God. Love the LORD your God with all your heart, with all your soul, and with all your strength. Never forget these commands that I am giving you today. Teach them to your children. Repeat them when you are at home and when you are away, when you are resting and when you are working.   *Deuteronomy 6:4-7 GNB*

INFANT BLESSING (CONTD)

A song, a poem, or a piece of music could be performed and the blessing for a baby's future on page 38 may be used.

The minister or soul friend reads from the Gospel according to St. Mark:

They brought children for Jesus to touch. The disciples rebuked them, but when Jesus saw this he was indignant, and said to them, 'Let the children come to me; do not try to stop them; for the kingdom of God belongs to such as these. I tell you, whoever does not accept the kingdom of God like a child will never enter it.' And he put his arms around them, laid his hands upon them, and blessed them.

Mark 10:13-16 NEB

A card with the words of Deuteronomy 6:4-7 may be given to the parents to be put above the child's bedroom door, and also a copy of a Gospel.

The minister or soul friend says:

We welcome N . . . as Jesus welcomed children. This book contains the good news of God's love. Read it, for it tells how you and your family may turn from evil, trust in Jesus Christ, and share in God's eternal purpose.

Gifts may be given.

Prayers may be said.

INFANT BLESSING (CONTD)

The Circling Prayer and Blessing

A candle may be lit and given to the mother. Everyone stands in a circle around the baby and its mother.

The minister or soul friend places a hand on the child's head and says:

Christ as a light illumine and guide you. Christ as a shield overshadow you. Christ under you; Christ over you; Christ beside you; Christ ahead of you; Christ within you. Christ in the heart of friend and stranger. Christ as your light, every day of your life.

All say: **Circle *her/him*, Lord, keep harm without**

Circle *her/him*, Lord, keep evil without

Circle *her/him*, Lord, keep strife without

Circle *her/him*, Lord, keep lies without

Circle *her/him*, Lord, keep hatred without.

Any individual may name something they wish to be kept without.

All say: **Circle *her/him*, Lord, keep peace within**

Circle *her/him*, Lord, keep love within

Circle *her/him*, Lord, keep trust within

Circle *her/him*, Lord, keep truth within

Circle *her/him*, Lord, keep good within.

Any individual may name something they wish to be kept within.

INFANT BLESSING (CONTD)

The minister or soul friend says one or all of the following prayers:

Father of love, accept the thanksgiving of these parents. May their spirits, lifted to you now in humble gratitude, always turn to you for help and strength. Give them wisdom, tenderness, and patience, to guide their child to know right from wrong.

Father, may N... and N... be to the other a strength in need, a comfort in sorrow, a companion in joy. Knit their wills together in your will, that they may live together in love, hope and peace all their days.

May you respect one another;
May the goodness of friendship grow in you;
May the love that covers a multitude of sins be upon you.

God's peace be with you, whatever you do;
God's light to guide you wherever you go;
God's goodness to fill you and help you to grow.

Silence, singing, music, dancing or feasting may follow.

WEDDING

These prayers may also be used on the anniversary of the wedding or at a service for the renewal of wedding vows.

Before the start of a wedding service

Open our eyes to your presence

Open our ears to your call

Open our hearts to your love.

After the entrance of the bride as she stands beside the groom

Most powerful Spirit of God

Come down upon us and bless us

From heaven

Where the ordinary is made glorious

And glory seems but ordinary.

Bathe us

With the brilliance

Of your light

Like dew.

Bible reading or talk

In Brittany a priest often leads the bridal couple in a walk around the person who will read the Gospel (from the Bible which the reader holds up). This is a symbol of the journey through life which they are about to begin together. It is a way of saying: We do not know where our journey will lead, but wherever it leads, God's Word will be central to it.

Before the vows

There may be a time of reflection focussing on the bride and groom, to the accompaniment of light pipes. During this anyone may write down prayers, sayings, or good wishes, or draw a picture on pieces of paper provided. Here is an example of a prayer that can be written out on a card and given or read out:

May the Father take you
In his fragrant clasp of love
In every up and every down of your life.

The love and affection of God be with you
The love and affection of the angels be with you
The love and affection of the saints in heaven be with you
The love and affection of your friends on earth be with you
To guard you
To cherish you
To bring you to your eternal fulfilment.

Joining hands after the vows

May you be bound with unbreakable bonds of love to one another
May you be bound with unbreakable bonds of love to your God
May your love for each other reflect the love
of your Maker, Saviour and Guide,
The Three of limitless love.

A bridal blessing after the vows

May the Father take you in his fragrant clasp of love
May the Virgin Mary's Son guide you through the maze of life
May the generous Spirit release forgiving love within you,
Hour by hour, by day and by night, in joy and in failure.
May all men and all women who are saints in heaven
Urge you on to complete your course.

WEDDING (CONTD)

Prayers

God's own presence with you stay
Jesus to shield you in the fray
Spirit to protect you from all ill
Trinity there guiding you still.

On sea or land, in ebb or flow,
God be with you wherever you go.
In flow or ebb, on land or sea
God's great might your protecting be.

Lord
let our memory
provide no shelter
for grievance against each other.

Lord
let our heart provide no harbour
for hatred of each other.

Lord
let our tongue
be no accomplice
in the judgment of each other.

*For the new household that the couple are to recreate in the
community:*

May you be host to the great High King,
with all the company of heaven.
The sustenance of pure love be in your house,
the roots of repentance in your house.
Baskets of love be yours to give,
with cups of mercy for all the company.
May sweet Jesus, and all the company of heaven, be there
with you.

WEDDING (CONTD)

Circling

Everyone, or invited persons, may form a circle around the newly-married couple and pray this blessing together:

Circle them, Lord
Keep love within, keep hate without
Circle them, Lord, keep faith within, keep mistrust without.
Circle them, Lord, keep light within, keep dark without.

Blessings

May the road rise to meet you.

May the wind be always at your back.

May the sun shine warm upon your face.

The rain fall soft upon your fields,

And until we meet again

May God hold you

In the hollow of his hand.

May the Sacred Three pour upon you mildly and generously more and more for ever.

The Reception

Think carefully about the place as well as the building for the reception. Celtic Christians have a strong sense of place. I witnessed a Breton marriage celebration at the top of Mount Dol. This combined in one place a sense of prayer (there was a chapel), a place for eating (there was a restaurant and picnic tables), a place for dancing and a beautiful view, all of which could be captured well in video or photographs.

III

DAILY AND SEASONAL

Daily Rituals

WASHING

I wash my face in the sun
In the nine rays of the sun
As Mary washed her Son
In the rich fermented milk.

Love be in my countenance,
Benevolence in my mind,
Dew of honey in my tongue
My breath as the incense.

Carmina Gadelica

MEALTIME BLESSINGS

May this food restore our strength,
give new energy to tired limbs, new thoughts to weary minds.
May this drink restore our souls,
give new vision to dry spirits, new warmth to cold hearts.
And once refreshed,
may we give new pleasure to you, who gives us all.

May the blessing of the five loaves and the two fishes
which God shared out among the five thousand, be ours.
May the King who did the sharing bless our sharing.

Bless, O Lord, this food we are about to eat; and we pray you,
O God, that it may be good for our body and soul;
and if there be any poor creature hungry or thirsty walking
along the road,
send them into us that we can share the food with them,
just as you share your gifts with all of us.

Bless us, O God, bless our food and our drink,
Since it is you who bought us at such great price,
save us from all evil.

MEALTIME BLESSINGS (CONTD)

Give us, O God of the nourishing meal,
Well-being to the body, the frame of the soul.
Give us, O God of the honey-sweet milk,
The sap and the savour of the fragrant farms.

Some have meat and cannot eat;
Some cannot eat that want it:
But we have meat and we can eat
Sae let the Lord be thankit!

Robert Burns, modernised

God in our waking, God in our speaking;
God in our cooking, God in our eating;
God in our laughing, God in our digesting;
God in our working, God in our resting.

MEALTIME BLESSINGS (CONTD)

May this food so fresh and fragrant
Call forth reverence for you.
As you give this strength to our perishable limbs,
So give us grace for our eternal lives.

Thanks to you for the abundance of food,
For the bounty of creation,
For all that is good.

In a world where so many are hungry,
May we eat this food with humble hearts;
In a world where so many are lonely,
May we share this friendship with joyful hearts.

Bless you, King of the universe,
For this sign of your tender care.
Bless you, King of this eating room
For this sign that you are here.
Bless you, Creator of all we eat;
Bless you, Saviour - you with us meet;
Bless you, Spirit who makes this sweet.

You who put beam in moon and sun,
You who put food in ear and herd,
You who put fish in stream and sea,
Put a grateful heart in me.

MEALTIME BLESSINGS (CONTD)

Blessed are you, High King of the universe,

It is of your goodness we have this food to eat and this wine to drink,

Blessed be you for ever!

Bless, O Lord, this food which we are about to eat for our bodily welfare.

May we be strengthened thereby to do your holy will.

Glory, praise and thanks to you, O God, for this food and our good health.

We also thank you for all the food and health for which we have not thanked you.

A thousand thanks to you, O God, who has given us this food for the body.

Grant us we ask you, who are so generous, eternal life.

AFTER FOOD

A thousand thanks to you, O King of the universe;

a thousand thanks to you, O Lord of grace,

for what you have given us since our birth,

and for what you will give us until the day of our death.

Thanks be to you, O God, praise be to you, O God,

Reverence be to you, O God, for all that you have given me.

As you have given physical life to earn me my worldly food,

So grant me eternal life to show forth your glory.

SLEEP

Sleep in peace
Sleep soundly
Sleep in love.
Weaver of dreams
Weave well in you as you sleep.

I lie down this night
Near the King of Life
Near Christ of the destitute
Near the Holy Spirit.
I lie down this night
with the angels
From the crown of my head
To the soles of my feet;
From the crown of my head
To the soles of my feet.

Carmina Gadelica

ᴆᴀʏᴛɪᴍᴇ

MORNING

Encircle my soul
In morning stillness
Scatter the shadows of fear

Be at my side in midday bustle
Weave through the knotwork of time

Talk to my heart
In teatime chatter
Speak through the discords of life

Lighten the load
Of incoming darkness
Glow like a star at midnight.

Jane M Mackichan

MORNING (CONTD)

I arise today
In the strength of the mighty Creator
In the strength of the rising Saviour
In the strength of the life-giving Spirit
In the strength of the mighty Three
Whose love is One.

I arise today
In the strength of the angels and archangels
In the strength of the prophets and apostles
In the strength of the martyrs and saints.

I arise today
In the strength of heaven and earth
In the strength of sun and moon
In the strength of fire and wind.

I arise today
In the strength of Christ's birth and baptism
In the strength of Christ's death and rising
In the strength of Christ's judgment to come.

MIDDAY

We draw aside at the heart of the day
To seek your face and watch and pray
Refresh us O Lord and close to us stay
When we leave here and go our way.

As with manna you fed your fleeing folk
Like much needed rain on the parched dry ground
Refresh us now as your name we invoke
Come like dew, in power, on us.

Andrew Dick, from a song by Kentigern the band

EVENING

Tonight, God of rest

As I lay down in bed

I rest:

my hopes	my fears
my longings	my thankfulness
my being	my non-being
my anxieties	my faith
my decisions	my indecisions
my work	my contemplation

that which is complete

that which is incomplete

my seeing	my darkness
my hearing	my deafness
my feeling	my hardness
my openness	my closedness
my past	my future

myself in God, the community of the Three in me.

Carole Parker (adapted)

NIGHT

May we rest this night in the stillness of your being.

O Radiant Dawn, splendour of eternal light,

come and shine on us

that we may sleep in the warmth of your radiance.

O Emmanuel, God with us, we will lie down with you and you
will lie down with us.

And the dawn shall come and so will your appearing

and we shall know as we are known

And in pleasure you will receive us.

Call forth this night bearers of your presence.

Call forth this night believers in your truth.

seasonal

NEW YEAR

God bless to me this year
Never vouchsafed to me before.
It is to bless your own Presence
that you have given me this moment, O Lord.

Bless to me my eye
And everything it shall see
Bless to me my neighbour
May my neighbour be a blessing to me.

Bless to me my household
and all who are dear to me
Bless to me my work and all that belongs to your
provision.

Give to me a clean heart
That I may not need to hide from you
One moment of this new year.

EASTER

May Christ rise in glory
Scattering the darkness before your path.

The Sun of suns,
the eye of the great God.
The eye of the King of Hosts,
is rising upon us,
gently and generously.
Welcome, glorious Son,
dawn of a new day.
Glory to you, Son of the Most High,
human face of God,
labouring with us, spending your life for us,
cross-bound to set us free.

Living One,
sword bright,
first and last,
banish all fear
from our hearts and minds.
Forgive us our sin.
On each of our dyings
shed your lovely light.
Bright face of God,
warmed by your glory,
may we run with joy to tell others
as you go ahead of us
into the world.

Kate McIlhagga

SUMMER

O, King of the Tree of Life,
The blossoms on the branches are your people,
The singing birds are your angels,
The whispering breeze is your Spirit.

O, King of the Tree of Life,
May the blossoms bring forth the sweetest fruit,
May the birds sing out the highest praise,
May your Spirit cover all with his gentle breath.

Carmina Gadelica

HARVEST

Here is a way of celebrating harvest with a silent blessing:

Build a Celtic-shaped cross (the cross with a circle round it) on the floor, using flowers, stones, fruit, greenery etc. Form a circle round this. All take seven steps slowly to the right, then turn to the centre, bend, pick up a harvest item, slowly offer this to God to a count of ten and replace it. Repeat. This becomes a form of corporate meditative prayer for harvest.

May God
who clothes the flowers
and feeds the birds of the sky,
who leads the lambs to pasture
and the deer to water,
who multiplied loaves and fishes
and changed water into wine
lead us
feed us
multiply us
and change us
until we reflect
the glory of our Creator
through all eternity.

HALLOWE'EN

God of time
God of dark
God of earth
God of heaven,
You are
Stronger than the elements,
Stronger than the shadows,
Stronger than the fears,
Stronger than human wills,
Stronger than the spirits,
Stronger than magic spells.

Your presence be our shield
The love of God to enfold us
The peace of God to still us
The Spirit of God to fill us
The saints of God to inspire us
The angels of God to guard us
This night, this winter, for ever.

CHRISTMAS

Child of Glory

Child of Mary

Born in the stable

The King of all

You came to our wasteland

In our place suffered

Draw near to us who to you call.

Bless to us this Day of Joy

Open to us Heaven's generous gates

Strengthen our hope

Revive our tired souls

'Til we sing the joys of your glory

With all the angels of heaven.

CHRISTMAS TREE

Bless, O Lord, this Christmas Tree,
all that goes on to it
and all that goes on around it.

May the decorations remind us to buy things in a spirit of
joy, thoughtfulness and generosity.

May the needles that fall to the ground make us mindful
of the needs of poor and homeless people the world over.

May the branches that point upwards lead us to wonder
and worship the Creator who came from heaven to earth
as a little child.

IV

JOURNEY
THROUGH LIFE

JOURNEY THROUGH LIFE

A human life is so precious, it calls out to be taken seriously. Each human life is a journey, and on this journey there are some important turning points. These need to be properly marked, so that we don't become confused or lost. We all need landmarks in order to make sense of our lives. In this section, a blessing is provided for significant turning points on our journey. These should help to transform each turning into a landmark.

Ancient Celtic people focussed on four stars that are the fourfold cloaks worn upon the circuit of life. The following is a Christian prayer that reflects this understanding.

Lord of the elements, give us a good journey through life

Lord of the Star of the East, give us a kindly birth

Lord of the Star of the South, give us a great love

Lord of the Star of the West, give us a quiet age

Lord of the Star of the North, give us a blest death.

ANNIVERSARIES

The joy of that day be in your face
The joy that made you grow in grace
The joy of memory be yours today
The joy of growth along the way
May you be joy to all who meet you
God's angels be always there to greet you
The circle of Christ around your neck
That day in heaven may you ne'er forget.
On this your anniversary
God give you the best of memories
Christ give you pardon for failings past
Spirit give friendship's fruit that lasts.

BIRTH

I know a woman who is a scientist and was an atheist - until the birth of her first baby, which flooded her with a sense of wonder at the miracle of new life. Most of us need to express this sense of wonder, but we do not always have the words to do so.

These blessings are inspired by prayers used in the Scottish highlands and islands. These people had a conviction that to look into the face of a newborn child is to see a reflection of God.

These prayers may be said by a midwife, relative, or friend on the day of birth or soon after. If others are present, they can say the 'Amen' which means 'Yes!'

The speaker says to the child:

The lovely likeness of the Lord is in your face

> *Three drops of warm water are poured on the baby's forehead, one during each of the first three sentences.*

A little drop of your Creator
On your forehead, precious one.

All   Amen

A little drop of your Saviour
On your forehead, precious one.

All   Amen

A little drop of your Saviour
On your forehead, precious one.

All   Amen

A little drop of your Guardian Spirit
On your forehead, precious one.

All   Amen

A little drop of the Three
to shield you from harm
To fill you with their virtue

All   Amen

BIRTHDAYS

This blessing may be written out and given to someone on their birthday. But do not neglect your own birthday. Why not light a candle and slowly, with time for reflection, say this blessing for yourself?

Joy of birth be yours today
Joy of memory be yours today
Joy of life be yours today
Joy of goodness be yours today
Joy of creation be yours today
Joy of friendship be yours today
Joy of giving be yours today
Joy of maturing be yours today
Joy of being known be yours today
Joy of self-knowing be yours today
Joy of Shepherd Father be yours today
Joy of Mary's Son be yours today
Joy of Friendly Spirit be yours today
Joy of eternal life be yours today
And for ever.

ᴅᴀʀᴋ ᴛɪᴍᴇꜱ

Take me under your protection O beloved angel of God,
just as the Lord of grace so ordained. Accompany me at
all times and protect me from worry and danger.

I ask for the Light of Light, the vision of the Trinity,
And the grace of patience in the face of injustice.

Life is but a passing shadow,
our stay here is but for a time.
But we will have good weather after the final raindrop.

O God, all powerful, you are my strength.
O Lord of all the world, my life is yours.
Whatever be your will, may it be done.

O Lord, give me your grace and your love, and I will be
safe for evermore.

DESPAIR

*Despair can be caused by crushing disappointments. Often, however, it
is caused by painful experiences that lie deeply buried under the surface
of our everyday consciousness. Sometimes, sanity-destroying flashbacks
bring these to mind.*

*If you get such a flash-back, focus on an image of Christ being crucified,
and say a blessing on yourself in this pit of despair.*

Christ of the agony
Christ of the bleeding
Christ racked and stretched out on the Tree

DESPAIR (CONTD)

I place upon you my own agony
I place upon you my bleeding heart
I place upon you my despair.

Take it
Break it
Re-make it.

Your Tree of death became the Tree of Life;
Give your blessing of life to me.

VICTIM OF CRIME

Into your loss
Come
O Being of Gift
O Being of Peace
O Being of Life eternal.

Into your threat
Come
O Being of Strength
O Being of Peace
O Being of Life eternal.

Into your despair
Come
O Being of Hope
O Being of Peace
O Being of Life eternal

Into your devastation
Come
O Being of Love
O Being of Peace
O Being of Life eternal.

DIVORCE

Grant me
acceptance of pain without bitterness
grieving for loss without blame
forgiveness for frailty without remorse
renewal of trust without fear.

Sadness and sin behind us be
Farewell to marriage, but friends let us be.
Bless our children in their hurts
Bless us as parents with our warts.

death

OF AN ENEMY

This soul did little good to me, O Lord,
But this soul was yours.

So to this soul I say:
I bless the day you were born
I bless your growing up
I bless you, even in your dark deeds
And I bless you, soul, at your end.

Travel to the God who transforms
Travel to the Arms so wide
Travel to the Spirit all generous.

ᴅᴇᴀᴛʜ

OF MYSELF

These prayers are suitable for occasions when life in me seems to be ebbing, or when I want to prepare myself, while in full strength, for my final journey from this life.

As you were there
Before my life's beginning
Be there again
At my journey's end.

As you were there
At my soul's shaping
Father, be there too,
At my soul's departing.

Saviour and Friend, how wonderful art Thou,
My companion upon the changeful way,
The comforter of its weariness,
My guide to the Eternal Town,
The welcome at its gate.

Hebridean Altars

I am going home with you, to your home, to your home;
I am going home with you, to your home of mercy.
I am going home with you, to your home, to your home;
I am going home with you, to the Fount of all the
blessings.

Carmina Gadelica, adapted

DEATH (CONTD)

Alone with none but you, my God,
I journey on my way.
What need I fear, when you are near,
O King of night and day?
More safe am I within your hand
Than if a host did round me stand.

My life I yield to your command,
And bow to your control;
In peaceful calm, for from your arm
No power can snatch my soul.
Could earthly foes ever appal
A soul that heeds the heavenly call!

Attributed to St. Columba

O great God of heaven, draw my soul to you;
Give to me sincere repentance.
O Healer of my soul, bestow on me forgiveness;
Give to me joy and gladness.
O great God of life, breathe through me your life,
Give to me strong Spirit of powers.
O gracious God of angels, bathe me in your light;
Give to me the loving spirit of the Lamb.

Echoes a prayer in Carmina Gadelica

My good angel, messenger of God,
Protect my body and my soul;
Protect me from the evil spirit
And above all else from sin.
I pray you, saints, men and women,
I pray you, Jesus,
To protect me and obtain for me
A good and happy death.

Brittany

ᴅᴇᴀᴛʜ
OF OTHERS WHO ARE WEAK OR DYING

As in the highlands and islands, blessings over a dying person may be said by an 'anamchara' (a soul friend) or by a minister or relative, with others. These death blessings are sometimes known as 'soul leading' or 'soul peace'. The soul peace should be said slowly (unless it is sung as in the Isles), all present joining the dying person in asking the Three Persons of the Trinity and the saints in heaven to receive the departing soul. During the prayer the soul friend, minister or relative makes the sign of the cross on the forehead of the the dying person (in the Isles it is made over the lips with the thumb).

Even with people who have little religious background, a well-known Bible passage, psalm or hymn (e.g. 'Abide with me') may be read, and one or more of the prayers that follow. A cross may be held in front of them.

Sleep, sleep, and away with sorrow,
Sleep in the arms of Jesus.
Sleep in the breast of virgin Mother,
Sleep in the calm of all calm,
Sleep in the love of all loves.
Sleep in the Lord of life eternal.

Carmina Gadelica, adapted

DEATH (CONTD)

May kindly Michael, Chief of the holy angels,
Take charge of your beloved soul,
And tenderly bring it home
To the Three of limitless love,
Creator, Saviour, Life-giver.

Carmina Gadelica, adapted

God be with you today and for ever
Jesus be in you to pardon and tether
Spirit be on you and leave you never.

The Circling Prayer

This may be used as a prayer for oneself using 'me' and 'my'.

The Holy Three encircle you
The Saving Three release you
The Eternal Three keep you
May the Loving Three caress you and work in you,
In your loved ones,
In those you have lost,
In your dark,
In your day,
In your pain,
In your seeing,
In your journey,
In eternity.

DEATH (CONTD)

In the name of the all-powerful Father,
In the name of the all-loving Son,
In the name of the all-pervading Spirit,
I command all spirit of fear to leave you,
I break the power of unforgiven sin in you,
I set you free from dependence upon human ties
That you may be
As free as the wind,
As soft as sheep's wool,
As straight as an arrow,
And that you may journey into the heart of God.

Death

OF AN UNBORN CHILD

The mother:

Dear God, the child (or children) who was/were lost through abortion is/are mine and yours.

Dear God, I am sorry that I have forgotten and ignored them. I ask their forgiveness and yours. It helps to know that no child is lost to you.

First, I wish to say I am especially sorry that the life of my ... *[first, second etc.]* child was taken through abortion. I am grateful, Lord, that you know all about the pressures, the difficulties and the problems that caused me to take that decision. Whatever my reasons, Lord, I am truly sorry for the taking of this life. I ask forgiveness from you and from the child who has died. I acknowledge before you that this was truly a child and was truly my own. I place this child into your tender care, I assure *him/her* of my love.

A minster or friend:

We release ... *[Name of aborted child]* into your hands. May your blessing and your peace be upon ... Bring *him/her* to wholeness in your eternal kingdom.

Parent:

Now, dear Jesus, I wish to name before you the one who was born on ... *[date]*. In faith I name *him/her* ...
I ask you to heal ... of any shock or hurt [s]he has carried as a result of the way [s]he died.

DEATH (CONTD)

Blessings on the parent by a soul friend or minister:

Lord Jesus, in your name we break the power of the past
to have a hold over N... May the cross of Christ come
between you and your past. The love of Jesus fill
you, a lamb of his choosing, that you may rest in his
arms, and walk free into the fruitful paths he has for you.

*A cross, flower, plant or plaque may be put in a place of
remembrance.*

Three drops of water may be poured on that spot,
using this prayer for a baby:

A little drop of your Creator, precious one.
A little drop of your Saviour, precious one
A little drop of your Guardian Spirit, precious one.
To bless you with virtue and sweetness,
To keep you in eternal life.

All Amen.

*There may be words of praise, encouragement or
singing. If desired, there may be the laying on of
hands in silent or spoken prayer.*

Blessing

May the tender and gracious God pour out love upon you
May you walk free and walk tall.
May the Creator's power protect you
The Saviour's care enfold you
The Spirit's life renew you.
May you walk in the fragrant clasp
of the Three of limitless love
now and for ever.

FALLING IN LOVE

The resurgence of interest in the legends of the Celtic King Arthur reflect a deep longing to discover a way of loving that has true romance, chivalry, and fidelity. It seems that, despite the widespread cheapening of sex, something deep in the human heart does not want it to be like that. The Arthurian myths can help young people who are growing up to visualise an alternative way of loving. But if this is to become a reality, this alternative way needs to be marked at the time when attraction to the opposite sex first awakens.

This blessing can also be written out and given to sons, daughters or friends at the time when they reveal their first romantic feelings.

Bless this thing that sparks like lightning
That burns like fire
That radiates like the inside of the first moment of the cosmos
In this awakening love may there always be
courtesy and respect
trust and courage
tenderness and truth.
Take from it all that destroys and is wilful
Give to it all that lasts and is selfless
That the one may wither and the other may grow strong
And shine for ever.
God bless this one whom I feel such love for.
May I never cheapen this love
May I never use the other just to gratify my appetites
May I always be there for the other
May this love be like a flower that slowly opens up to
reveal its full beauty
May I offer my beloved a heart of valour, restraint, and service.

LEAVING HOME

May God look after you wherever you go
May the everlasting Father take you in his generous clasp
May Christ lead you to your true destination
May the Spirit bathe you in heavenly light.

May the saints and the angels stretch out their arms for you
When you are tempted
When you go through rough places
When you return home.

The peace of the Son of peace be with you
And your children's children
Each day and each night
Of your life in this world.

MANHOOD: A BOY'S FIRST STEPS

In most societies, when a boy reaches puberty, he is weaned from his mother, and his father or his father's peers take him off to face the world outside of the home, to learn to tackle things, to work, to stand on his own feet.

In our society, too, it is possible to mark this stage for a boy or a girl. A father, or a leader in a local organisation or church might take the youngster away for an activity weekend. Before he leaves, or later, a parent might place their hands on his shoulders or head, and give a blessing such as the following.

God help you to:

run straight

speak what is true

ask questions

overcome fear

learn self-control

bear failure

stand alone

care for your body

guard your soul

honour women

respect men

explore the world

give your best

open your heart to all people

close your heart to all pretence

know yourself

reverence the Creator

walk with the Saviour

flow with the Spirit

enter into your eternal destiny.

MID-LIFE CRISIS

Life passes by?
Blessing of letting go be yours.

Fear of losing out?
Blessing of lowly spirit be yours.

Driven by false ambition?
Blessing of having nothing be yours.

Flight from chaos within?
Blessing of true being be yours.

Anger at failing before others?
Blessing of eternal reward be yours.

Weary of time-worn patterns?
Blessing of dawn be yours.

Losing faith in your peers?
Blessing of angels be yours.

Disillusioned even with life?
Blessing of resurrection be yours.

OLD AGE

This blessing reflects Psalm 92:4

May you be evergreen and full of sap
and bear fruit each day of your life.

*Celtic people were impressed by the fact that three trees - holly, mistletoe
and yew - kept their leaves green throughout the year. They thought
that these symbolised certain things in human lives that were meant to
remain evergreen, even if other parts of life fell away in old age. This
blessing reflects that insight.*

As holly, mistletoe and yew
keep their leaves green throughout the year
so may these three things
be kept evergreen in you -
respect, restraint, and reverence for life.

*I once came across a prayer for middle age written by a Carmelite nun.
This inspired the following blessing for someone who is beginning to
grow old.*

God keep you from
having to say something on every occasion,
having to sort out everyone else's affairs,
reciting endless details.
God give you wings to get to the point.

OLD AGE (CONTD)

God seal your lips on your aches and pains.

God keep you reasonably sweet,
for a sour old person is one of the crowning works of the devil.

God help you to endure with patience others' tales of woe.

God give you
an ability to see good things in unexpected places,
talents in unexpected people,
and the grace to tell them so.

God
keep you from evil within,
shield you from evil without,
bless you with virtue and sweetness,
aid you in times of trial.

God
give you pluck and valour,
bring you good health and good speech,
save you for good and for God,
the One and the Three who is love.

RETIREMENT

Wisdom of years be yours
Joy of friendships be yours
Wealth of memories be yours
Fruit of endeavour be yours
Hope of heaven be yours
Peace of God be yours.

REUNIONS

The welcome of the Father's arms be yours
The welcome of the Saviour's heart be yours
The welcome of the Spirit's call be yours.

Deep peace of this earth to you
Deep peace of this sky to you
Deep peace of this place to you.

The kindly eye of the Three be upon you
To aid you and guard you
To cherish and enrich you.

May God take you in the clasp of his own two hands.

school
GOING TO SCHOOL

May smiling faces welcome you
May helping hands welcome you
May kind teachers welcome you

May
fears fly away
temper go away
lies stay away.

May you
make new friends
learn new things
grow strong limbs.

May
God make you thoughtful
Jesus make you happy
Spirit make you friendly.

AT SCHOOL

Lord, circle this school
and keep these good things within:

eagerness to learn
flowering of talents
a sense of wonder
enjoyment of sport
experience of beauty
warmth of friendship
the art of listening
respect for all
service of others
teamwork between children and adults
care for the planet
reverence for life
fitness of body, mind and spirit.

AT SCHOOL (CONTD)

Lord, circle this school
and keep these bad things without:

> low self-esteem
> confusion
> prejudice
> pride
> bullying
> cheating
> stealing
> fear of appraisal
> malicious gossip
> absenteeism
> 'couldn't care less' attitudes.

Lord, circle this school
for you are the source of all that is good and true.
Amen.

LEAVING SCHOOL

Dear God
I've come to the end of my school years
with mixed feelings.
As I look back
And as I look to what is coming,
I see all sorts of shapes and colours
In flow and flux.
God of shapes and colours
Bless these to me
And be in the flow and flux

LEAVING SCHOOL (CONTD)

As I look back
And as I look to what is coming,
I see all sorts of empty gaps
In flux and flow.
God of the gaps
Fill these for me
And be in the flux and flow.

As I look back
Bless me with forgiveness
And the knowledge that
Nothing need be wasted with you.

As I look forward
How can I find out what work is right for me?
Bless my questioning and finding out.
Will I get a job?
Bless to me my work
All the talents you have put within me
May they grow wherever I shall be.

Be a vision to guide me
A voice to lead me
A Saviour to forgive me
A hand to hold me
A friend to teach me
Always.

WOMANHOOD: A GIRL'S FIRST PERIOD

This is a blessing of the God of life
The blessing of mild mother Mary
From whose breasts our Lord suckled milk.

May God give you strength in every such time
May Christ give you love in every such time
May Spirit give you peace in every such time.

Lord, place these nine choice graces
in the upturned face
of this day's wakened lass:
the grace of deportment
the grace of voice
the grace of provision
the grace of goodness
the grace of wisdom
the grace of caring
the grace of femininity
the grace of a lovely personality
the grace of godly speech.

fiNALLY

May everything in you be blessed;
and may you bless every one
and every thing.

May you be bathed in the blessings
that the Great Blesser
delights to shower upon you.

May you be saved from the sourness
that corrodes the person
who neglects to bless.

Bring forth buds of hope
Bring fruitfulness to this stagnant earth
May flowers and beauty bloom on it
May friendships grow on it
May songs burst forth
And dancing, loving, creating after stagnant barren years.

The blessing of God and the Lord be yours,
The blessing of the perfect Spirit be yours,
The blessing of the Three be pouring on you
mildly and generously, more and more
and for ever.

ACKNOWLEDGMENTS & SOURCES

Many of the prayers in this book echo blessings in the *Carmina Gadelica* collected and translated into English by Alexander Carmichael. Published by Floris Books, Edinburgh, 1992.

Many of the mealtime blessings echo those in *Traditional Irish Prayers* collected and translated into English by Paidrecha Ilghneitheacha and published by Mount Melleray Abbey, Waterford, Eire.

Some of the prayers for the sick and for baptism were previously published as separate sheets by the Community of Aidan and Hilda.

The prayers 'Bless the car ...' on page 28 and 'Tonight, God of rest ...' on page 74 are copyright Carole Parker, first published in *The Aidan Way* the magazine of The Community of Aidan and Hilda c/o Lindisfarne Retreat, Holy Island, Berwick-upon-Tweed TD15 2SD.

I am indebted to Keith Hitchman for some suggestions for the wedding blessings.

The wedding prayers 'Most powerful Spirit of God' and 'Lord, let our memory provide no shelter' are from *Celtic Night Prayer* published by HarperCollins © 1996 The Northumbria Community Trust and used with permission; 'God's own presence with you stay' is by David Adam.

The Easter Blessing 'Glory to you' is copyright Kate McIlhagga and is from *Encompassing Presence*, the Prayer Handbook for 1993 published by the United Reformed Church in the UK.

I would also like to thank the following for the use of their prayers:
Andrew Dick for his adaptation of my prayer in the song by Kentigern 'We draw aside at the heart of the day . . .' on p. 71;

Jane M. Mackichan for her prayer 'In the stillness . . .' on p. 3 and 'Encircle my soul' on p. 71;

Craig Roberts for his prayer 'As I look at their leaves'
on p. 26;

USA Festival of Names Church for the prayer 'In blessing our
foreheads . . .' on p. 33;

Esther de Waal for her prayer 'I programme my computer . . .'
on p. 3.